Tom Martinson

There's No Such Thing as
Identical Twins

A Civic Handbook for Community Leaders

In memory of Ronald L. Tulis, 1946-2008

Tom Martinson

© 2011 Two Worlds Community Foundation
7550 East McDonald Drive . Suite A
Scottsdale, Arizona 85250
Telephone 480.991.1942

Cover and book design by Pao Cagnina
ISBN 978-0-615-59932-8

CONTENTS

Introduction 1

Community Wholeness 5

Municipal Cycles 13

City Stages 19

Consistency 25

Building on the Past 31

Responses 40

References 42

INTRODUCTION

Someone once calculated that an architect makes about 50,000 decisions between beginning a house design and homeowner move-in. That's just for one house. Imagine how many separate choices underlie the development of a neighborhood, much less the growth of an entire metropolitan area.

Thinking about your neighborhood and region in that light, you can appreciate that there are almost infinite possible permutations of community planning choices—the responses to any particular location and its climate, physical features, local economy, social traditions, design opportunities, and many other influential variables.

So each community reflects the current sum of an uncountable number of decisions made over decades by public bodies, stakeholders, and generations of residents. It follows that every neighborhood differs in its issues and potentials, indeed in its very essence, from all others. As I like to think of it, there's no such thing as identical twins.

You would never know that from today's city-planning conventions. Considering the extraordinary diverseness among American cities, suburbs, and towns, it's amazing, if not embarrassing, how shallow our reigning neighborhood-development theories are. One generic ideology fits all. If you are a public official, a civic leader, or active in community affairs, you know what I mean. Community-planning prescriptions are pretty much the same from coast to coast: houses must have front porches set next to public sidewalks. Subdivisions should have tiny lots, and be laid out in a regular street grid with alleys—cul-de-sacs are beyond the pale. People of all ages and physical conditions (and daily schedules) are to walk or bike everywhere, especially to a rail-transit stop. As a signature town-planning ideal, everyone should live within a ten-minute walk of a store selling ice-cream cones. Really. I am not making this up.

Never mind that, say, Houston is Amazon-torrid half the year and Minneapolis is Siberia the other half. Neither is exactly front-porch-friendly, even if residents of both cities weren't inside evenings watching TV like the rest of America. Or that people love living on cul-de-sacs, because with no through traffic it is safer for their children, and quieter for themselves. Many Americans do walk and ride bikes for exercise, but outside of New York City and a handful of other big cities, few commute on foot or by (wildly expensive) rail transit. And of course we can walk to our freezer in ten *seconds* for that ice-cream cone.

Responding to a Radically Changing America

Believe me, I could go on and on, but the deficiencies of the present state of city and town planning are obvious enough. We desperately need effective approaches to building and maintaining our communities. The Great Recession marks a sweeping break from the past, the way the Second World War separated Depression-era American life from the radically different postwar America. Derivative planning fashions featuring front porches do not offer constructive directions for a difficult future that demands invention.

Planning must acknowledge the inherent potentials of each neighborhood from founding to maturity, and beyond. Naturally solutions have to respond creatively to the actual situation, not merely impose a standardized ideology about how everyone should live, everywhere.

This handbook is intended to support your efforts to improve your own community. The following themed chapters introduce useful ways of evaluating your choices. Over four decades of community-development planning throughout the United States and large-scale projects across East Asia, I've devised a number of planning tools for my clients which may also be helpful to you.

First, here are three guiding insights that have proved themselves in my city-planning experience. They are: Every situation is unique. Every solution should be creative. And balance is usually good.

Every Situation is Unique

One of my colleagues described a well-known architectural firm in a perceptive shorthand. This highly successful international practice had garnered hundreds of design awards for their projects. But precious few of the firm's designs fit happily into their setting. As a consequence, while their evident technical skills were impressive, you rarely loved being in and around the firm's buildings. My colleague explained this emotional disconnect from building users and lack of sympathy with the surroundings by noting that, "They are very good at supplying answers. They just don't ask many questions."

In my experience, asking relevant up-front questions is fundamental to successfully building and revitalizing our communities. We need to ask enough questions to fully understand a locality's particular problems and to appreciate its specific potentials before devising planning solutions. That is because every situation is unique. There's no such thing as identical twins.

Every Solution Should be Creative

This insight should be unremarkable. That it is not says volumes about the values that we apply to our communities. "Creative" has long been put down in real-estate-development circles as meaning "artistic" and thus "not practical." This allows property developers to justify following their same old formula again and again as efficient and responsible. They usually get away with it because public officials have two overriding political goals, *in this order*: 1. To not look bad; and 2. To look good. Creative as it has been misdefined implies a risk of looking bad.

Yet if you recognize Webster's definitions of creative as "imaginative" and "inventive", then you can appreciate why every community-development solution should be creative. Who would want to live in a boring neighborhood if the alternative was an imaginative one? And given today's radically changing society, we constantly need inventive ideas about what we should do. Community leaders must insist that in these challenging times, simply not looking bad is not good enough.

Balance is Usually Good

Balance is central to achieving community harmony. That should come as no surprise, since balance seems to be the default setting of the universe, whether as described by Newton's Laws of Motion or implied by the Golden Rule.

To be sure, being out of balance can sometimes be considered a plus: think of a gritty urban quarter that is alluring to thrill seekers because of its edginess; or of a brilliant artist whose genius pushes her to live well outside of society's norms.

Nevertheless, most communities, as most people, benefit from maintaining a sense of balance. That is why offering a few stand-out civic features usually cannot compensate for a mass of municipal shortcomings. A treasure trove of landmark architecture and magnificent public spaces will be less-attractive if the neighborhood is wracked by crime. Community pride about a perennially winning high-school football program is tempered if the school perennially ranks low academically.

Anyone who has looked for housing in several different neighborhoods appreciates the importance of these kinds of reservations and tradeoffs. So we continue the discussion of balance, and its sibling, wholeness, in the next chapter.

COMMUNITY WHOLENESS

How, exactly, is a community whole? And why should it matter?

Over years of planning practice, I've noticed that attractive communities are typically characterized by a balanced array of public and private attributes. That is a key reason why they are desirable places to live. Easy enough to note the obvious!

It is a little more difficult to explain how this actually comes about, and to define what that all entails. Because every situation is unique, because there are no identical twins, the particular mix of attributes which supports any community's balance and wholeness will also be unique, since "community" is always a custom creation.

Maslow's Classic Human Needs Hierarchy

That said, I've found it useful to consider the nature of community wholeness as adapted from Maslow's 1943 basic-needs hierarchy, a staple of psychology texts. In this theory psychologist Abraham Maslow proposed a hierarchy of human needs. These are summarized on the left half of the following chart. Maslow's needs hierarchy begins at a fundamental level, with our life-or-death requirements for air, water, and food.

Subsequent levels identify human needs for psychological safety, emotional connections, and self-esteem. At an ultimate level, some people (though not all, according to Maslow) need an outlet for creative self-fulfillment. Although the theory cannot be proved, it is broadly acknowledged by psychologists.

Maslow's Human Needs Hierarchy

Fundamental Level: **Physiological Needs**
    air, water, food

Second Level: **Safety needs**
    Stability and protection; freedom from fear, anxiety and
    chaos; structure, order and fairly applied law

Third Level: **Belongingness and Love Needs**
    A general hunger for relations with people, giving and
    receiving affection

Fourth Level: **Esteem Needs**
    Personal confidence based on competence, achievement,
    and status; afforded presige; experiencing attention and
    appreciation

Ultimate Level: **Self-actualization Needs** (Not univeral)
    Creative self-fulfillment; what the individual can be s/
    he must be; making music, painting, athletic success,
    inventing things

There's No Such Thing as Identical Twins

Community Needs Hierarchy

Fundamental Level: **Shelter and Income**
> Wide range of available and affordable housing types; full range of employment opportunities

Second Level: **Public Order**
> Secure, healthful environment; ease of movement and assessibility; schools; responsive government

Third Level: **Connections and Tolerance**
> Pleasant interrelationships with neighbors; community acceptance; abundant community and religious activities

Fourth Level: **Civic Expressions**
> Widely shared community standards; distinctiveness; festivals, shaping the local landscape; the achievement of beauty

Ultimate Level: **Design Expressions** (Not universal)
> Creative expressions: architecture, landscape architecture, public art, performing arts

Maslow included two essential insights along with his theory:

First, each need level is more essential to the individual than are subsequent levels.

Second, if a more-basic need becomes unfulfilled, the individual's focus will unavoidably fall back to the more-basic level until that need is once again satisfied.

When you think about it, these two insights make perfect sense. For instance, someone who is starving (fundamental need level) will probably not attempt much creative self-fulfillment (ultimate need level) until he has regained a reliable source of meals.

Maslow's theory sounds like the ancient proverb about not building on shifting sands. To fully participate in society's rich banquet of opportunities, an individual benefits from a stable physical foundation and emotional security.

A Community Needs Hierarchy

This notion of building from stable foundations can be applied to the community as well as to the individual. A community-needs analogy with Maslow's human-needs hierarchy is depicted on the right half of the chart. Just as air, water, and food are essential to the body, shelter and income are fundamental needs in modern society. Without shelter, there is no place to live. Without income, there is no means of support.

Next, comparable to an individual's safety needs, is the community's need for public order. Neighborhoods must be safe and healthful. People must be able to get from here to there. Schools must be provided. Government should be effective, and responsive to its citizens.

Maslow's third-level belongingness and love needs for the individual correspond to a community characterized by consideration, connections, and tolerance. The singular neighbor relationship requires sensitivity to how a person's own lifestyle impacts those living nearby. Openness toward people of all

There's No Such Thing as Identical Twins

races and beliefs will deepen one's pool of potential friendships. A wealth of local social activities and religious institutions expands social contacts throughout the entire community.

At a fourth level, the individual's esteem needs correspond to the community's civic expressions. This is what the community says about itself. What unwritten, home-grown societal standards prevail? What is unique about the community, and how is that evident in local traditions? Is there broad-based participation in community celebrations? How closely does the built environment integrate with the natural environment? Is the community's visual environment more attractive than was the unimproved landscape before development began?

Finally, for some communities there is an ultimate level of design expressions, of formal creativity. This may manifest in signature architecture, citywide expressions of landscape architecture, in public art, and in regular opportunities to both participate in and attend performing-arts events. At a deeper level, University of California Berkeley architecture professor Marc Treib observed that design expressions ideally build from memory that transmits the unique aspects of a locality's culture and history.

These five need levels suggest how communities can be whole. This is an illustrative guideline; it does not assert a particular mix of specific ingredients which are best for all communities, of course. Every situation is unique, after all.

The community-needs hierarchy also parallels Maslow's hierarchy with respect to the primacy of basic levels over subsequent levels. Shelter and income do indeed come first. People are less-likely to participate in civic celebrations (fourth level) if there is a breakdown in public order (second level). Design expressions (ultimate level) will probably ring hollow for many of us wherever human connections and tolerance (third level) are missing.

Both Visual and Non-visual Attributes

As a physical planner, I find this all very useful. The insight for me is that balanced, harmonious communities benefit from a locally derived mix of many distinct attributes, *not all (or even most) of which are visual.* Some of these will be more important to any particular community's residents than are others. A neighborhood in which all (or at least the first four levels) of these attributes are consistently present is more likely to feel whole to its residents. Those communities in which only a scattering of such attributes are present, especially if not beginning at the fundamental level, can be thought of as incomplete. They would not be experienced as especially harmonious, and thus might seem less desirable.

Whether a neighborhood is whole or incomplete could explain, for instance, why one person living in a sparkling new planned development might be discontented, while another treasures her nondescript postwar subdivision.

The planned community might offer distinctive architecture and beautiful landscaping, but perhaps strong neighborhood relationships have not had time to develop, and lasting civic traditions have not yet emerged. So at present it cannot be fully experienced as an authentic place.

In contrast, the nondescript subdivision might not look like much to outsiders. It may be one of those "cookie cutter" developments scorned by design critics. Regardless, large numbers of modest-income Americans are elated just to live in their own house, and this mature neighborhood has developed a lively social life, including civic traditions that are meaningful to residents. In short, it is a neighborhood with stable foundations, and is a good place to live. This resonates with people for whom the most important measure of their community is simply whether they are comfortable in their everyday life.

Understandably, we tend to judge communities and their individual neighborhoods by how they look. But that does not necessarily tell us if residents are content living there. Some people may indeed be satisfied by a single visual feature—say, an architecturally significant town center or an ocean view. For many others of us, though, our personal ideals can only be fulfilled through a combination of subjective experiences, especially human interrelationships, which together provide a sense of wholeness. These sum up as simply whether we enjoy living how and where we do in a balanced, harmonious setting.

There's No Such Thing as Identical Twins

MUNICIPAL CYCLES

When I graduated from college in the mid-1960s, my home town of Minneapolis was a miracle of planning activity. Downtown planning. Redevelopment planning. Neighborhood planning. Large-scale special-district plans.

These were not just paper plans, mind you. They were action agendas guiding dozens of projects then underway. Entire neighborhoods were revitalized, as was the landmark park system. Spectacular architecture became the new norm. Downtown's now-iconic 70-block pedestrian "skyway" system was invented. What an exhilarating place to live and work for a young physical planner like myself.

By the 1970s Minneapolis was literally a city transformed from what it had been a little over a decade earlier. Minnesota—Minneapolis, really—graced the cover of *Time*. The city-planning department regularly received delegations from as far away as Japan intent on learning the city's secret. During this period, you might recall, New York City was tottering on the abyss of municipal bankruptcy.

What a difference a generation makes. New York City "came back" big time by the 1990s, as we all know. Meanwhile Minneapolis quietly receded from the national scene, with subsequent media attention lavished on the likes of Denver, Portland, and Seattle. Minneapolis' heroic mid-century civic era is clearly long over.

What insight are we to draw from this abbreviated tale of two cities? The very short answer is that it illustrates municipal cycles.

Communities *can* achieve their highest potentials. Just not at any time. American social history and the built legacies of its prominent cities reveal a continuous ebb-and-flow of visionary civic activity extending back to before the Revolution. For any successful city, eras marked by impressive public achievements are interspersed with periods of inattention to even long-festering matters. Such down times are characterized by a decided lack of innovative municipal activity.

The specific situation and thus timing of any local civic era are, of course, unique for each city. That explains the apparent decline of New York City when Minneapolis was flying high. And the later resurgence of New York City, especially Manhattan, by when inventive civic achievement in Minneapolis was but a pale shadow of its earlier state. Notwithstanding national economic cycles and periodic Washington political realignments, some city or another is a potential hotbed of visionary innovation at almost any time.

I should add that this ebb-and-flow of creative civic undertaking is not a bad thing. Heroic civic eras are exhilarating. But they are also exhausting for their participants. Moreover, cities need time to consolidate their gains after a period of great accomplishment. This usually requires an entirely different kind of public and private leadership, with a visionary civic generation succeeded by pragmatic implementers.

Crucibles

A crucible is defined as "a severe test," and that pretty well describes what usually stimulates a heroic civic era. A community's leadership must be challenged. But here is a key proviso: the challenge must consist of both serious problems to be solved *and* exceptional unrealized potentials which are realistically within reach. Local leaders rightly need a reward for their commitment. Great civic achievement is a reward commensurate with their necessary dedication over years.

We can imagine a wide range of conditions that would

be crucibles. On one extreme are Rustbelt cities which have been shattered by massive plant closings. Such a community definitely has searing problems. Yet without a healthy local economy and cohesive business leadership, it is unlikely to experience a renaissance. So there would be no psychic-emotional reward for local leaders after years of fruitless civic commitment. Instead, purely municipal mitigations like a demolition program for blighted properties and job retraining might be the most effective course for this city.

Phoenix occupies the other extreme. The Valley of the Sun is without doubt a crucible, its numerous pressing issues regularly reported by the nation's media. But many of these problems are brought on by strong growth. And growth is a sign of attractiveness. So there is upside economic and thus civic potential here, unlike our Rustbelt example.

In addition, because Phoenix is unburdened by obsolete prewar development patterns, and since local civic leadership is untraditional and fluid, the city and region currently enjoy great potential for breakthrough visionary achievements.

Local Leadership

Specific accomplishments among communities vary from minor to extraordinary, and vary as well in the timing of civic undertakings. These observed variations are largely explained by the qualities of local civic-public leadership combined with the strength of the local economy.

To place this in context, probably less than ten-percent of all American pioneer settlements are still fully functioning communities. That means all of today's stable municipalities have overcome daunting odds just to remain in existence. These cities and towns can be appreciated at one of three levels of success, beyond mere survival. At a basic level, functioning communities by definition offer an array of basic goods and services like groceries, doctor and dentist, auto repair, churches, and schools.

Beyond this fundamental level, a small percentage of municipalities additionally offer institutions such as hospitals, colleges, and museums, and an expanded array of commerce and services perhaps including scheduled air service. The leadership of these "second-level" communities is characteristically more aggressive and persistent than the leadership of "first-level" functioning communities.

At a third level, a very small number of American municipalities have creatively exploited their own singular potentials, like the distinctive historical setting of Charleston, South Carolina and the imaginative Riverwalk in San Antonio. Remarkable environments like these are the result of visionary civic and public leadership. Unique local qualities energize and color a community's singular personality: this is why they are especially appealing places to live, and to visit.

"Third level" communities which effectively focus on their own potentials probably enjoy high qualities of local leadership and *civic continuity*. These places are more likely to be balanced and whole. In the United States, visionary civic leadership commonly occurs in three forms:

Golden-era Leadership—Some American cities have enjoyed exceptional civic accomplishment during a single era. These exciting times are marked by a confluence of exceptional leaders and a then-powerful local economy. If leadership in later cycles is not visionary and the local economy declines, this golden era will prove to be a one-time peak of civic activity.

As an example, Buffalo enjoyed exceptional public and private achievements between the 1870s and about 1920, a period when the city was a dynamic global leader in grain milling. That era is recalled by the city's marvelous physical artifacts, including Frederic Law Olmsted's park system and the splendid turn-of-the-century downtown fabric, which is still largely intact.

There's No Such Thing as Identical Twins

Similarly, Butte's vivid downtown core attests to its epic "zenith" age of a century ago. However, lacking later comparable accomplishments, golden-era communities may read today as curiously left in the past.

Recurring Leadership—Other American cities have experienced multiple peak cycles of visionary civic attainment, separated by periods of routine activity. Minneapolis enjoyed singular achievements during three peak eras: initially during its entrepreneurial pioneer industrial activities of the 1870s and 1880s; then the development of its unique park system in the prewar twentieth century; and finally (so far, at least) the stunning transformation of its downtown and neighborhoods in the 1960s and early 1970s noted at the chapter beginning.

While impressive in and of themselves, such recurring accomplishments function, visually and symbolically, as isolated, ad hoc episodes in the city's development history. If civic undertakings are not grounded in a larger idea about the city itself, they do not offer the synergies that accrue to enhancements that build, over generations, toward a cohesive community expression.

Consistent Leadership—A few American cities and towns *are* grounded in a local self-image that consistently guides their civic undertakings—generation after generation of public officials and civic leaders fully appreciate what is "right" for their community.

Sometimes this larger idea is as uncomplicated as a signature visual character, like Santa Barbara reinventing itself as the American Riviera, consistently expressed since the 1920s in Spanish Colonial Revival architectural imageries.

In a more complex appreciation, St. Louis's traditional self image as a national public city has informed the community in many ways over the past century, including a consistent emphasis on monumental public spaces and landmark public buildings. The city's ultimate civic symbol, Gateway Arch, is the product of sixty years of continuous civic and political advocacy.

Consistently holding to a guiding self image makes it much more likely that every individual enhancement will strengthen a community's common civic expression, thus continuously reinforcing its singular personality and attractiveness. Hence the ideal community leadership is characterized by continuity in appreciating what should be done, and persistence, over several generations if necessary, in accomplishing that goal.

CITY STAGES

As American cities mature, they pass through a succession of stages, each marked by distinct leadership styles and community-development approaches. The following chart illustrates one generalized progression of these stages as observed over the past half century.

This evolution is linear, not cyclical. Cities in any of these stages may or may not have experienced visionary civic achievements as outlined in the previous chapter.

In and of itself, the following chart is mildly interesting. Most of us will try and locate our own community and probably find that it does not fit precisely within any one of the stages as depicted on the chart. Cities are constantly evolving, usually unevenly, and one or two attributes might be changing more rapidly than others.

The chart's real value is what you can usefully read into it. Both for American cities in general and specifically for your own community.

For instance, since being a mature city is desirable, but facing persistent urban dysfunction is not, what can be done to prevent maturing cities—*your* maturing city—from inevitably declining into a state of dysfunction, instead of continuously enhancing their singular qualities and attractiveness like, for example, Boston?

A related question: is there something about public decision-making and reinvestment choices common to mature American cities that places them at particular risk of decline? Or is it that most cities do whatever most other cities are doing, rather than focusing on their own unique potentials and thus, their inherent attractiveness?

Developing City	rapidly-growing postwar suburbia / 1950s Dallas
Emphasis:	private construction
Investment:	infrastructure and public facilities
Condition:	"holes" but little blight
Reinvestement:	few if any remedial programs
Leadership:	intuitive municipal decisions and/or influential private "inner circle"

Transitional Stage	maturing suburbs / 1970s Minneapolis
Emphasis:	largely built-out; focus shifts to infill construction
Investment:	special projects, cultural and sports facilities, designed housing
Condition:	physical and demographic decline in older districts
Reinvestement:	experimental and scattered remedial programs
Leadership:	extensive policy planning; often-exhaustive public hearings, task forces

Mature City	1980s St. Louis
Emphasis:	economic development
Investment:	protection of/fallback to the commercial core
Condition:	noticeable physical, social decline beyond fringes and amenity districts
Reinvestement:	directed remedial programs
Leadership:	slow consensus-building, citizen resistance to change

Persistent Urban Dysfunction	New Orleans
Emphasis:	little consistent emphasis; reacts to small number of private proposals
Investment:	cope with decay
Condition:	widespread decline, though can be domain of rich and poor
Reinvestement:	de facto triage; fallow districts
Leadership:	inconsistent municipal decisions, diminished citizen expectations

There's No Such Thing as Identical Twins

At local scale, if your community seems to be scattered across these stages, it may signal that its leadership hasn't established a clear course. Though it could be that your community is in the process of creatively breaking conventions, and is growing ever-more balanced, whole, and uniquely attractive as a result.

Suggesting a Direction; Not a Blueprint

One additional thought about the chart: it summarizes common planning experience over the last half of the twentieth century. In addition to serving as history, the chart can also serve as background for future decisions—although only up to a point. Right now these leadership styles and community-development approaches seem timeless, and thus instructive in illustrating a direction which your own community might follow.

Yet every era is ultimately singular in important respects.

Inevitably, then, successful responses to the future evolution of American communities may well differ in significant ways from those past responses depicted on the chart.

For instance, a century ago new laws empowering business corporations, a relative lack of regulations, and technologies like telephones and elevators led to a concentration of national business activity in major downtowns, so that movers and shakers could profit from routine face-to-face contact. Today, newer laws, anti-trust regulations limiting agreements if not contact among competitors, and advanced communication technologies have brought about the opposite effect: business activity has decentralized, as corporations merge and move headquarters across the continent, scattering back-office jobs to "business-friendly" states, if they are not already outsourced to other countries. All we can reliably count on is that Times Change.

Yesterday, Today, and Tomorrow

In addition to wholeness, attractive communities large and small are similar in two respects. First, they appreciate and celebrate what makes them unique. And second, they consistently capitalize on those unique qualities no matter what any other community does, and regardless of planning fashion.

This implies that community planning should ideally extend the influence of time, beyond only working in the present. Since cities effectively exist forever, the present is merely one arbitrary spot on an endless timeline, a snapshot that is constantly moving onward. To fully exploit the civic potentials of this reality, a community's planning should seamlessly address the past, the present, and the future:

Completing the Past—Memory is the currency of great cities. Every progressive community has initiatives left unfinished by previous generations of civic leaders that may or may not be remembered by the current generation. These could be undertakings dating from recent years or might be proposals made decades ago. Doubtless some of these were deservedly not followed up! But others could have been brilliant ideas left unfulfilled for reasons which no longer apply. Completing historic initiatives capitalizes on good locally focused ideas, precious for any community. Doing so will also deepen a community's sense of time and enhance underlying local traditions.

Representing the Present—Of course we live in the present, so it is important to inventively solve current problems and take creative advantage of current opportunities. How well we do so is a reflection of ourselves, how history will remember the civic contributions of our generation.

Seeding the Future—Continuity extends forward. Many, perhaps most communities harbor visionary potentials that are not addressed because they cannot reasonably be completed at this time. However a strong concept, perhaps physically demonstrated at manageable scale, can provide a seed for future generations to grow, and eventually harvest. Iconic concepts like the two-miles-long Gateway Mall in St. Louis and the Minneapolis Grand Rounds park system have taken generations to accomplish; indeed, Gateway Mall is still underway after more than a century of patient development

The Evolving Nature of Community

Probably most of us unconsciously assume that American cities will always be pretty much like those in our own experience. Now of course New York City is very different from Los Angeles, but both regions can be encompassed under this handbook, even if they don't share the same issues and opportunities.

Though from a longer perspective we can see that over several-hundred years of Europeanization, the character, daily life, problems, and potentials of American towns and cities have continuously evolved. The pre-industrial Manhattan of 1800, for instance, was very different from the Manhattan emerging as a manufacturing-business center in 1900. The nature of corporate postwar Manhattan was very different from its current global-finance manifestation.

So we should expect that the nature of community will continue to evolve, changing radically at times. Take for instance the multiple virtual communities which make up today's Silicon Valley. As described by *The New York Times* writer Steve Lohr in 2007, virtual tech communities are forming around flagship IT companies, based on "industry niches, skills, school ties, traffic patterns, ethnic groups, and even weekend sports teams."

Few IT product-design and engineering startups now locate in Palo Alto, the historic center of Silicon Valley. Rather they find office space near Google's headquarters if they are oriented to the Internet; close to Intel if their focus is on chips; or around Cisco if they are developing networking technologies. In another technology sector, Internet marketing and social networking startups favor high-style San Francisco as a location over nerd-dominated Silicon Valley.

These companies establish de facto communities comprised of engineers and their families, in the process eroding our conventional geographic presumption about community as where you physically live. While people will still have to live somewhere, community allegiances in the future could be focused in more than one place, presenting new opportunities for both "bedroom" and "active" locations.

Hence understanding past city stage as a way of anticipating future city stages is very important to successfully shaping our communities.

CONSISTENCY

Over the years I've noticed that some cities are remarkably consistent in how they understand and express themselves—following the consistent-leadership model cited in the Municipal Cycles chapter. This noteworthy ability strengthens a city's unique personality.

Communities marked by consistency are impressively realistic in playing to their strengths. Meaning that they explicitly recognize those strengths. Hence they are able to reinforce those strengths through both public and private ventures, generation after generation. The resulting synergies enhance the collective value of those ventures by more than the sum of the individual undertakings.

I think of this internalized understanding as the community's expectation for itself, reflecting its unique civic self-image. Yet another confirmation that there's no such thing as identical twins.

These consistently clear-eyed cities unmistakably project any of four distinct expectations, as depicted on the following chart. I label these as Functional, Systematic, Innovative, and Global. Please do not think of these categories as hierarchical. A global city, for instance, is not inherently better than a city reliably guided by functional expectations. "Better" for any community is simply whatever resonates as authentic for the citizens of that particular community.

Also, there seems to be no typical path to a particular expectation. The cities serving as examples on the chart (along with many others enjoying similar consistency) each arrived at their characteristic expectation in their own way.

Expectation	Examples	Emphasis	Expression
Functional "Market-driven"	**Omaha Seoul**	Infrastructure	Facilities
Systematic "City That Works"	**Minneapolis Singapore**	Systems	Architecture
Innovative "National City"	**St. Louis Vancouver**	Environments	Landscapes
Global "World City"	**San Fransico Paris**	Experiences	Human Activity

All four of these civic self-images are found to some extent in every major American city. No city, not even a single city neighborhood, is 100-percent shaped by just one of these expectations. There are always outliers. Municipal consistency is a matter of one expectation manifesting significantly stronger than any of the other three, evident in everything from local founding myths to cultural venues to municipal investments.

However this one-expectation emphasis is not hard-and-fast. As an example, postwar Minneapolis has consistently acted as a systematic city, notably in employing architecture as a signature civic expression. Yet the city's magnificent Grand Rounds park system (dating in concept from 1891) ranks among the great American civic landscape environments. This century-old innovative tradition in Minneapolis coexists in parallel with the city's mostly systematic public and private undertakings of the past half century.

Strong-and-consistent parallel expectations like those of Minneapolis are unusual. It is more common in systematic, innovative, and global cities that utilitarian public works and routine private developments are treated as functional matters, while civic undertakings and important private projects follow the underlying community expectation. As long as this

There's No Such Thing as Identical Twins

occurs fairly dependably, a succession of significant public and private improvements will probably build toward an outcome that is greater than the sums of the individual improvements, enhancing the community's attractiveness.

Alas, many cities are inconsistent to a fault. No single expectation is especially prominent in their public and private undertakings. As a result, the physical environment sends out mixed messages, contributing to what some observers describe as a feeling of placelessness.

Functional—Functional cities exhibit a pervasive practical streak, emphasizing stability and reliability. Local private-investment decisions are understood to be market-driven, while public undertakings focus on no-nonsense dependability. Symbolic civic projects are few-and-far-between, rarely if ever grand in expression. Of course reliability is a virtue. That is how Omaha capitalized on the massive Cold War infrastructure investment for the Strategic Air Command Omaha headquarters, by successfully promoting its extensive local communications capacity into an early center of telemarketing, fitting the skills of a good part of its workforce.

Following a totally unrelated path (than Omaha's) to its similar expectation, Seoul had little choice but to focus on function because of staggering growth. From a population of less than one-million at the end of the Second World War, the region more than doubled in population by 1960, grew by an additional 250-percent over the next decade, and by now has more than ten-million residents. Seoul's endless miles of concrete apartment blocks were a practical, cost-efficient response to unprecedented demands for housing. While outsider might consider Seoul's housing to be visually brutal living environments, South Koreans had to survive two decades of truly brutal hardship caused by war. For that reason alone, the environmental esthetics of the city's postwar housing was clearly not a significant consideration, given the city's necessarily functional expectation.

Systematic—Systematic cities like postwar Minneapolis and post-1965 Singapore (when the city-state became an independent nation) pursue a civic goal of putting it all together, taking pride in building a City That Works. Advanced interrelated infrastructure especially differentiates systematic cities from functional cities, which simply provide infrastructure.

As illustrations, Minneapolis developed a comprehensive downtown movement system by seamlessly integrating freeways, peripheral parking, and climate-controlled pedestrian skywalks. Singapore pioneered congestion-reducing traffic management though a layer of vehicle tolls based on time of the day and district.

Perhaps because advanced technical solutions are rarely visually interesting, systematic cities tend to emphasize dramatic architecture as signature civic symbols. Tellingly, these are typically private office towers; signature public constructions are characteristic of cities holding innovative and global expectations.

Systematic cities are usually much more aggressive about establishing their presence than are functional cities (which given their practical orientation, are content to be left on their own). When you hear or read about an improvement that local civic leaders tout as "world class," that is a tip-off that you are probably in a systematic city.

Innovative—Cities like St. Louis and Vancouver sharply differ from systematic cities in their self-centeredness. They are strongly inward-focused, relatively unconcerned about how others might judge them, compared to aggressive systematic cities. Even so, innovative cities are quite aware of their prominent national cultural role, and so they concentrate on developing an appropriately singular setting reflecting their symbolic leadership status.

Because they understand themselves as role models, innovative cities are less-likely than systematic cities to do what everyone else is doing. Hence, innovative cities tend to emphasize large-scale physical environments as signature civic symbols. In the case of Vancouver's splendid natural setting, this can be primarily a matter of thoughtful conservation of preserves, edges, and views. St. Louis has developed its Gateway Mall, planned to extend about two miles back from the Mississippi riverfront, as a unique public landscape reflecting the city's historic role as a national gateway to western expansion.

Global—World cities like San Francisco and Paris are much more than the mere sums of their individual attractions, buildings, and landscapes. They are total experiences. Visitors and residents respond not just to a physical place but to a palpable ambiance. These two representative global cities offer architecture, monumental landscapes and streetscapes, museums, restaurants, shopping, and much more.

Even so, human activity is arguably the most memorable local feature. If you played a word-association game with "Paris," for instance, the immediate response from many people might well be "sidewalk cafés." Importantly, this appealing human activity is qualitative, since there are many places throughout the world where the streetscape is overrun with people. If just any kind of human activity was the measure, then Calcutta would be a much-more-attractive experience than Paris or San Francisco.

Global cities vary widely in their physical qualities: there is little direct comparison between, say, Rome and Cairo, of course. Two characteristics are common among all, however. One is that they are experiences even more than they are environments, however visually memorable. The other is that world culture cannot be fully described without reference to these singular places.

In our diverse United States, some of us will be attracted to cities of each expectation, and no expectation will be appealing to everyone. While San Francisco is a magnificent living experience to millions of regional residents, it is too crowded and expensive to be attractive as a home for millions of others.

The message of this chapter is to highlight the importance of every community truly knowing itself, acting consistently on that knowledge.

BUILDING ON THE PAST

Ambivalence toward the past is a characteristically American attitude. After all, the premise that America is the future is deeply ingrained in our national myths, attracting millions of immigrants seeking a fresh start.

Countering this forward-looking mindset, many Americans do indeed look back to an imagined golden era for reassurance. And with respect to American built environments, a golden past is hardly imaginary: exceptional designs and landscapes are found throughout the country, beginning with ancient aboriginal sites and extraordinary Pueblo constructions dating from well more than a millennia ago.

Now as a practical matter, ambivalence about something this significant cannot be a good thing. That is why it is necessary for communities to come to terms with their past. Because each community differs from all others, every community's relationship to the past is singular. Moreover, there are several differing perspectives about preserving the past, any of which may or may not be relevant to the situation in a particular community. These are identified in the chart, "Traditional Perspectives on Historic Preservation."

Perspectives on the Past

As illustrated by the chart, the past can be appreciated from multiple points of view. Consistently applied locally, any one of these perspectives would lead to a distinctly different outcome in a community, compared to the likely outcomes from consistently following any of the others.

So it is essential that each community decides which of these perspectives is most relevant to its own situation. This includes not just the character of physical fabric, but also appreciating local social values and traditions.

Antiquarian—Some people just like old things. From such a perspective, it would be ideal if we could stop time! Though of course since change is inevitable, this is not a realistic goal for dynamic American communities.

Absent the possibility of stopping time, antiquarian preservationists hope to slow down change as much as possible. This can be accomplished by establishing historic districts, the larger the better, even imposing informal restrictions on nearby areas not within a district on the grounds that changes there would materially impact the district itself.

Ironically, New York City, which to most of us is the very definition of dynamic, has designated more than 23,000 (not a typo) properties and districts as historic and protected. As a result, a significant amount of the city's developed land is controlled, with new construction effectively limited in character by a municipal landmarks commission.

An antiquarian approach to the past can be valuable in preserving very old and architecturally cohesive townscapes like Deerfield, Massachusetts. However, this approach diminishes, if not eliminates the potential for new construction and remodeling to authentically reflect their own time. As a consequence, a community governed by an antiquarian perspective will grow increasingly derivative in character.

Romantic—A romantic differs from an antiquarian in taking a discriminating view of the past, appreciating creative qualities over mere age. So a romantic perspective unsurprisingly focuses on architectural and historic landmarks, and visually superior districts.

Romantics are the classic historic preservationists, responsible for saving priceless sites like Monticello and Mount Vernon in the nineteenth century, and for the twentieth-century restoration-rebuilding of Colonial Williamsburg. James Biddle, the last resident of his ancestral 1830s landmark estate, Andalusia, and long-time president of the National Trust for Historic Preservation, represented the epitome of a romantic perspective.

A romantic approach can be especially valuable for communities with a substantial inventory of significant architecture, in identifying and preserving exceptional local historic fabric. In terms of practical local politics, this perspective is easier to explain (than is the antiquarian perspective) to those who are not especially enamored with the past—in some places and eras, a majority of citizens—since the intrinsic creative qualities of the landmark buildings and sites appreciated by romantics are usually evident to everyone.

Because of its relatively narrow focus on design quality, unlike the much broader antiquarian outlook, a romantic approach to historic preservation will usually reduce the total land area with restrictions on contemporary building, compared to a community following antiquarian instincts. This should increase the community's potentials for gaining authentically contemporary designs in the future.

On the down side, a classic romantic perspective may not always fully appreciate buildings and sites outside of a high-design mainstream, including, for instance, representative vernacular buildings and recent designs.

Authority—This perspective on the past is the domain of professionals: architects with grounding in historic buildings and PhD architectural historians and cultural historians. Authorities recognize an endless timeline of past, present, and future which has produced authentic contemporary constructions all along the way. They appreciate the characteristic expressions of every past era, while also documenting significant contemporary work.

Authorities are found throughout academia, especially in institutions with architecture programs; and at elite levels of the federal government, notably within the National Park Service. Authorities established the Historic American Buildings Survey, the professional standards for which provided the underlying basis for the National Register program (which itself was the legislative product of authorities, in 1966). Charles Peterson, an architect who founded HABS in the mid-1930s, was the father of authorities in the United States.

Authorities can be important resources for communities, both for their capacity to sort through subjective appraisals and also for their professional stature, especially in instances where historic designations or refusals to designate are contentious issues, subject to legal challenges. Authorities can undertake complex designation studies like those for the Georgetown section of Washington, D.C. beginning in the mid-1960s.

Rationalist—A rational view toward the past is associated with physical planners like Edmund Bacon, Philadelphia's planning director in the 1950s and 1960s during its celebrated Center City planning. Bacon authored the classic book, Design of Cities (1967).

Quite the opposite from antiquarians, for whom historic fabric is perceived as a separate entity to be protected from change, rationalist planners seek to seamlessly integrate historic buildings and landscapes into the endless timeline—past, present, and future—of a community's physical fabric.

A rationalist especially values the way historic buildings and sites impart a sense of visual depth, a palpable indication of time, into a townscape/cityscape. Historic properties ideally read as integral parts of the overall community fabric, as in European cities, rather than as protected, freestanding sites that are visually, or at least symbolically, set apart from the surrounding community.

The rationalist is likely to be even-more-discerning than the romantic with respect to historic designations, emphasizing the best representative buildings, sites, and landscapes. Rationalist physical planners are essential to a community wishing to organically incorporate its landmark physical fabric.

Realist—Like any real property, historic buildings and sites require financial support. Acquisition, rehabilitation-restoration, operations, and continuing maintenance cost money. Comparatively few historic sites can be economically carried as museums, supported solely through admissions and donations. Fortunately from a public-finance perspective, most historic houses are entrusted to homeowners, many of whom must accommodate special restrictions imposed by local ordinances on historic properties.

Non-residential historic properties are dependent on the small subset of property developers who appreciate the potentials of old buildings and have the expertise and patience, including deep pockets, to undertake improvements to structures considered by conventional markets to be obsolete. An exceptional national example is the visually astonishing, financially intimidating Glenwood Mission Inn in Riverside, California, whose restoration was initially undertaken by the visionary developer David Carley.

Even much-less-complex projects than Mission Inn are difficult, since municipalities usually impose additional layers of conditions on the development of historic structures; approvals are uncertain even after substantial investment on the parts of developers; and lenders are consequently uneasy about such undertakings. Not surprisingly, many historic properties remain in decline, passed over by investors-developers.

To increase local private investment in historic properties, communities can take three actions to reduce uncertainty. First, public officials and staff should thoroughly understand the process from a developer's point of view. This should reduce the unrealistic demands often placed on developers of historic properties.

Second, the municipality should clearly set out its objective *and subjective* expectations up front, so that developers are not blindsided by new requirements well down the line. And third, many communities need to revisit their approvals process to ensure that all important issues are addressed in the most efficient and economical way.

Other Perspectives on the Past

In addition to the widespread perspectives identified in the chart, the past is frequently cited from other perspectives. Three of the most common are identified here:

Environmental—An environmentalist appreciates the built environment as a resource already in place. Why tear down existing buildings? They represent investments in energy and materials that will be lost if demolished—and then even-more energy and materials will be required to rebuild the site. Where old structures are torn down, the environmentalist calls for the reuse of building materials to the greatest degree possible, from wood flooring to architectural ornament.

This is a compelling and responsible position. Even so, it is not always financially defensible. A developer operating from a realist perspective will observe that many old structures are functionally obsolete to the extent that they are uneconomical to reuse. And even when a building can be rehabilitated, the local market may not appreciate it enough to fully lease up. The realist-developer will also note that recycling building materials is highly labor-intensive, and thus might be economically problematic.

Urban Design—Historic-preservation ordinances are often employed as a stand-in for what are really urban-design issues. Into the 1970s, professionally trained architects-urban designers were prominent on municipal planning department staffs. They developed comprehensive physical plans which focused on the community's fabric; historic sites and buildings were understood as one integral planning component among several.

Since the 1970s urban-designer professionals have been succeeded by administrators-regulators in most planning departments, in cities and suburbs alike. As a consequence, little background design study, much less conceptual direction, is available to elected officials when visual issues arise, as they regularly do. So citizens invoke historic-preservation ordinances in order to deal with underlying urban-design issues such as building height, texture, view corridors, pedestrian movement, and traffic circulation. Of course it would be more effective if communities addressed their physical-visual situation comprehensively, instead of through a succession of ad-hoc controversies.

Activist—Historic Preservation is invoked by activists to stop private projects and public improvements. While this approach is also employed by antiquarians, the activist is not necessarily committed to preserving old things, as the antiquarian truly is. Rather, historic-preservation ordinances are applied by the activist as convenient political tools, with the side benefit of appearing to be selflessly on the side of angels in preserving the community's heritage.

Employment of the past is useful to Not In My Back Yard activists in augmenting their political leverage under existing public-hearing laws. Though if the past is misused as a ruse, public support for genuine historic-preservation actions may weaken as a consequence.

To communities, sufficiently acknowledging the past clearly requires much more than designating historic buildings for protection. Every community is presented with a wide range of choices of how to come to terms with its past. Which ones are best for any given situation can only be decided locally. But they must be decided.

• This chart identifies five distinct perspectives on preservation. Into the 1970s, designation was primarily the domain of architects and architectural historians—"authorities." Today's typical preservation administrators do not necessarily share these values, any more than, say, a county administrator would closely appreciate the legal rulings of the courts nominally under his/her responsibility.

• Historic Preservation has passed through several eras of typical emphasis, beginning with national significance (Mount Vernon, New Orleans French Quarter) through mid-century; high art (Frank Lloyd Wright, state capitols) into the 1970s; expanding into popular culture (diners, gas stations); engineering (highways, bridges, industrial); and marine. The recent focus seems to be everyday-ordinary, ranging from visually undistinguished farm houses to conventional subdivisions that "typify" common developments.

• This flight from distinction to the ordinary has been facilitated by a diminishment of the influence of professional architectural historians and a rise of preservation administrators. While historic designations still go through the motions of assessing importance, virtually anything can now qualify as "exemplify[ing] the broad trends of . . . history."

• As represented by Richard Moe, the former president of the National Trust for Historic Preservation who succeeded James Biddle, preservation's traditional cultural emphasis has now been superseded by an openly political movement, locally and nationally. There is nothing wrong with a political movement, of course. Still, the underlying historic-preservation enabling laws are based on the presumption that designations are to be made on the basis of intrinsic quality and representative significance.

There's No Such Thing as Identical Twins

TRADITIONAL PERSPECTIVES ON HISTORIC PRESERVATION

ANTIQUARIAN	ROMANTIC	AUTHORITY	RATIONALIST	REALIST
Likes old things; buildings should be preserved and sites conserved simply because of their age	Cherishes the way things used to be; prefers older buildings because they were "better"	Appreciates exceptional qualities of buildings and sites; best buildings saved as models; intrinsic value	Sees value in visual mix of old and new, many eras and styles; retain best representative buildings	Properties must function economically; reuse old buildings where unique or if market demands
•Historical Societies •Genealogies •Colonial Dames	•"Committee for the Preservation of . . ." •1949 National Trust	• 1934 Historic American Buildings Survey •1966 NHP Act: Nat Reg	•Downtown reinvestment •Neighborhood revitalization	•Prewar industrial rehabs •Class-C commercial office rehabilitations
Bed & Breakfast	Williamsburg	Georgetown D.C.	Center City Philadelphia	Glenwood Mission Inn
Narrative Historian	**Classic Preservationist**	**Architectural Historian**	**City Planner**	**Property Developer**
Local history buff	James Biddle	Charles Peterson	Edmund Bacon	David Carley

RESPONSES

If you take away just one insight from this handbook, I hope you'll think of those non-identical twins. When you appreciate that your community differs from all others, you will also appreciate why every solution needs to be customized to its setting.

By all means look around to see what other cities are doing. But whenever something afar catches your attention, be sure to temper your enthusiasm with the knowledge that whatever works really well elsewhere authentically responds to the actual issues and opportunities in that elsewhere. Your community's most-successful civic undertakings will necessarily differ.

The planning tools in this book are intended as orientation, and to help ground your custom approach to a better community. If this reading has stirred new ideas about how you might proceed, I'll consider the book a success.

Now comes the fun part. All those permutations of decisions noted in the introduction mean that you face a myriad of choices. What should you consider? On what basis?

With such questions we have moved into the next stage in the community-development process, responses to your community's situation. These are colored by many influences, from climate to local design attitudes.

Thoroughly addressing each of these possible responses often requires attention at a surprising level of detail. For instance, to understand the influences of climate, in addition to temperatures you will want to consider the effects of seasonality, sunlight, precipitation, wind, and storms. Each of these may have several aspects, for example in the case of seasonality, changing sun angles, seasonal horticulture, seasonal color, and winter.

Fear not, I will not leave you in the lurch. There is more to come on responses in my next handbook, *A Myriad of Choices*, from the Two Worlds Community Foundation.

Tom Martinson

August, 2011

REFERENCES

Allen, Frederick Lewis. The Big Change: America Transforms Itself, 1900-1950 (1952). Westport, CT: Greenwood Press Publishers, 1983.

Bacon, Edmund N. Design of Cities. New York: Viking Press, 1967.

Beatley, Timothy. Green Urbanism: Learning From European Cities. Washington, D.C.: Island Press, 2000.

Bernick, Michael, and Robert Cervero. Transit Villages in the 21st Century. New York: McGraw-Hill, 1997.

Beverage, Charles E., and Paul Rocheleau. Frederick Law Olmsted: Designing the American Landscape. New York: Rizzoli, 1995.

Birnbaum, Charles A., and Robin Karson. Pioneers of American Landscape Design. New York: McGraw-Hill, 2000.

Brown, David, et. al., eds. Sustainable Architecture White Papers. New York: Earth Pledge Foundation, 2000.

Bruegmann, Robert. Sprawl: A Compact History. Chicago: The University of Chicago Press, 2005.

Bugeja, Michael. Interpersonal Divide: The Search for Community in a Technological Age. New York: Oxford University Press, 2005.

Burnham, Daniel H., and Edward H. Bennett. Plan of Chicago. Chicago: The Commercial Club, 1909.

Calthorpe, Peter, and William Fulton. The Regional City: Planning for the End of Sprawl. Washington, D.C.: Island Press, 2001.

Caro, Robert A. The Power Broker: Robert Moses and the Fall of New York. New York: Vintage Books, (1974) 1975.

Clark, Robert Judson. Design in America: The Cranbrook Vision 1925-1950. New York: Harry N. Abrams, 1983.

Corner, James and Alex S. MacLean. Taking Measure Across the American Landscape. New Haven: Yale University Press, 1996.

Crouch, Dora P., Daniel J. Garr, and Axel Mundigo. Spanish City Planning in

North America. Cambridge: The MIT Press, 1982.

Duany, Andres, Elizabeth Plater-Zyberk, and Jeff Speck. Suburban Nation: The Rise of Sprawl and the Decline of the American Dream. New York: North Point Press, 2000.

Eckbo, Garrett. Landscape For Living. New York: Duell, Sloan, & Pearce, 1950.

Ehrenhalt, Alan. The Lost City: Discovering the Forgotten Virtues of Community in the Chicago of the 1950s. New York: Basic Books, 1995.

Fogelson, Robert M. Downtown: Its Rise and Fall, 1880-1950. New Haven: Yale University Press, 2001.

Frantz, Douglas, and Catherine Collins. Celebration, U.S.A.: Living in Disney's Brave New Town. New York: Henry Holt and Company, 1999.

Gans, Herbert J. The Levittowners: Ways of Life and Politics in a New Suburban Community. New York: Pantheon Books/Random House, 1967.

Garreau, Joel. Edge City: Life on the New Frontier New York: Doubleday, 1991.

Gottmann, Jean. Megalopolis: The Urbanized Northeastern Seaboard of the United States. New York: The Twentieth Century Fund, 1961.

Grogan, Paul S., and Tony Proscio. Comeback Cities: A Blueprint for Urban Neighborhood Revival. Boulder, CO: Westview Press, 2000.

Jackson, John Brinckerhoff. A Sense of Place, A Sense of Time. New Haven: Yale University Press, 1994.

Jasper, James M. Restless Nation: Starting Over in America. Chicago: The University of Chicago Press, 2000.

Johnson, Hildegard Binder. Order Upon the Land: The U.S. Rectangular Land Survey and the Upper Mississippi Country. New York: Oxford University Press, 1976.

Kamin, Blair. Why Architecture Matters: Lessons from Chicago. Chicago: University of Chicago Press, 2001.

Kaplan, Robert D. An Empire Wilderness: Travels Into America's Future. New York: Vintage Books, 1998.

Kirp, David. Almost Home: America's Love-Hate Relationship With Community. Princeton: Princeton University Press, 2000.

Kostof, Spiro. A History of Architecture: Settings and Rituals. New York: Oxford University Press, 1985.

Kotkin, Joel. The New Geography: How the Digital Revolution is Reshaping the American Landscape. New York: Random House, 2000.

Lai, Richard Tseng-yu. Law in Urban Design and Planning: The Invisible Web. New York: Van Nostrand Reinhold Company, 1988.

Langdon, Philip. A Better Place to Live: Reshaping the American Suburb. Amherst: The University of Massachusetts Press, 1994.

Leepson, Marc. Saving Monticello: The Levy Family's Epic Quest to Rescue the House That Jefferson Built. New York: The Free Press, 2001.

Linklater, Andro. Measuring America: How an Untamed Wilderness Shaped the United States and Fulfilled the Promise of Democracy. New York: Walker & Company, 2002.

Lohr, Steve. "A Social Order Shaped By Technology and Traffic," The New York Times, December 20, 2007, pp. C1, C5.

Louv, Richard. America II. Los Angeles: Jeremy P. Tarcher, 1983.

Lynes, Russell. The Tastemakers: The Shaping of American Popular Taste (1954). New York: Dover Publications, 1980.

Martin, Frank Edgerton, and Kelly O'Brien. Documenting the Ordinary: The Suburban Documentation Project. (1990 ff) www.hhmuseum.org.

Martinson, Tom. American Dreamscape: The Pursuit of Happiness in Postwar Suburbia. New York: Carroll & Graf, 2000.

Martinson, Tom. The Atlas of American Architecture: 2000 Years of Architecture, City Planning, Landscape Architecture, and Civil Engineering. New York: Rizzoli, 2009.

Martinson, Tom. "The Persistence of Vision: A Century of Civic Progress in St. Louis." Places: A Quarterly Journal of Environmental Design, Summer 1990:22-33.

Maslow, Abraham H. Motivation and Personality (1954). New York: HarperCollinsPublishers, 1987.

McHarg, Ian L. Design With Nature. Garden City: The Natural History Press, 1969.

McHarg, Ian L. A Quest for Life: An Autobiography. New York: John Wiley & Sons, 1996.

McHarg, Ian L. and Frederick R. Steiner. To Heal the Earth: Selected Writings of Ian L. McHarg. Washington, D.C.: Island Press, 1998.

Miller, Donald L. Lewis Mumford: A Life. New York: Weidenfeld & Nicholson,

1989.

Mohney, David, and Keller Easterling, eds. Seaside: Making a Town in America. New York: Princeton Architectural Press, 1991.

Moore, Charles, Gerald Allen, and Donlyn Lyndon. The Place of Houses (1974). Berkeley: University of California Press, 2000.

Moore, Charles W. Water And Architecture. New York: Harry N. Abrams, 1994.

Moore, Charles W., William J. Mitchell, and William Turnbull, Jr. The Poetics of Gardens. Cambridge: The MIT Press, 1988.

Nolen, John. New Ideals in the Planning of Cities, Towns and Villages. New York City: American City Bureau, 1919.

Nolen, John. New Towns For Old: Achievements in Civic Improvements In Some American Small Towns And Neighborhoods. Boston: Marshall Jones Company, 1927.

Oehme, Wolfgang, James Van Sweden, with Susan Rademacher. Bold Romantic Gardens: The New World Landscapes of Oehme and van Sweden. Washington, D.C.: Spacemaker Press, 1998.

Oldenburg, Ray. The Great Good Place: Cafés, coffee shops, community centers, beauty parlors, general stores, bars, hangouts and how they get you through the day. New York: Paragon House, 1989.

Owens, Bill. Suburbia (1973). New York: Photofolio, 1999.

Pink, Daniel H. Free Agent Nation: How America's New Independent Workers Are Transforming the Way We Live. New York: Warner Books, 2001.

Reps, John W. The Making of Urban America: A History of City Planning in the United States. Princeton: Princeton University Press, 1965.

Reps, John W. Cities of the American West: A History of Frontier Urban Planning. Princeton: Princeton University Press, 1979.

Rogers, Elizabeth Barlow. Landscape Design: A Cultural and Architectural History. New York: Harry N. Abrams, 2001.

Ross, Andrew. The Celebration Chronicles: Life, Liberty, And The Pursuit Of Property Value In Disney's New Town. New York: Ballantine Books, 1999.

Roth, Marissa and D. J. Waldie. Real City: Downtown Los Angeles Inside/Out. Santa Monica: Angel City Press, 2001.

Rusk, David. Cities Without Suburbs. Washington, D.C.: The Woodrow Wilson

Center Press, 1993.

Russo, David J. American Towns: An Interpretive History. Chicago: Ivan R. Dee, 2001.

Rykwert, Joseph. The Seduction of Place: The City in the Twenty-first Century. New York: Pantheon Books, 2000.

Scott, Mel. American City Planning Since 1890. Berkeley: University of California Press, 1969.

Segal, Jerome M. Graceful Simplicity: Toward a Philosophy and Politics of Simple Living. New York: Henry Holt and Company, 1999.

Strauss, William and Neil Howe. The Fourth Turning: An American Prophecy. New York: Broadway Books, 1997.

Suarez, Ray. The Old Neighborhood: What We Lost in the Great Suburban Migration, 1966-1999. New York: Free Press, 1999.

Sullivan, Chip. Garden and Climate. New York: McGraw-Hill Companies, 2002.

Swaback, Vernon D., Designing For Living: Society's Greatest Challenge. Scottsdale: Two Worlds Community Foundation, 2011.

Swaback, Vernon D. Designing The Future. Tempe: Herberger Center for Design Excellence, 1997.

Swaback, Vernon D., Living in Two Worlds: The Creative Path to Community. Scottsdale: Two Worlds Community Foundation, 2010.

Swaback, Vernon D. The Custom Home. Mulgrave, Victoria, Australia: The Images Publishing Group, 2001.

Swaback, Vernon D. The Creative Community: Designing for Life. Mulgrave, Victoria, Australia: The Images Publishing Group, 2003.

Swaback, Vernon D. Creating Value: Smart Development and Green Design. Washington, D.C.: ULI Press, 2007.

Treib, Marc, and Dorothée Imbert. Garrett Eckbo: Modern Landscapes for Living. Berkeley: University of California Press, 1997.

Treib, Marc, ed. The Architecture of Landscape 1940-1960. Philadelphia: University of Pennsylvania Press, 2002.

Tung, Anthony M. Preserving the World's Great Cities :The Destruction and Renewal of the Historic Metropolis. New York: Clarkson Potter Publishers, 2001.

Urbanska, Wanda, and Frank Levering. Moving to a Small Town: A Guidebook for Moving from Urban to Rural America. New York: Fireside Books, 1996.

Waldie, D. J. Holy Land: A Suburban Memoir. New York: W. W. Norton & Company, 1996.

Whyte, William, H. The Social Life of Small Urban Spaces. Washington, D.C.: The Conservation Foundation, 1980.

Winter, Robert, ed. Toward A Simpler Way of Life: The Arts & Crafts Architects of California. Berkeley: Norfleet Press/University of California Press, 1997.

Wirth, Theodore. Minneapolis Park System: 1883-1944. Minneapolis: Board of Park Commissioners, 1946.

Wright, Frank Lloyd. An Autobiography. New York: Duell, Sloan and Pearce, 1943

Wright, Frank Lloyd. The Disappearing City. New York: William Farquhar Payson, 1932.

Wright, Frank Lloyd. The Living City. New York: Horizon Press, 1958.

Wright, Frank Lloyd. The Natural House. New York: Horizon Press, 1954.

Wright, Gwendolyn. Building the American Dream: A Social History of Housing in America. New York: Pantheon Books, 1981.